How many mice make an ELEPHANT?

and OTHEr BIG QUESTIons ABout SIZe and Distance

By
Tracey Turner

With Some Notes About Numbers by Kjartan Poskitt

Illustrated by Aaron Cushley

KINGFISHER

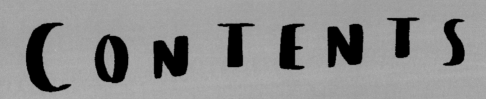

CONTENTS

Introduction

Have you ever wondered...

...just how big an elephant is?

Or how many flights of stairs it would take to climb Mount Everest?

Well, help is at hand, because we're about to find out. On the way, we'll...

...scale the world's tallest building using giraffes

...squash a lot of astronauts inside the International Space Station

...fill a stadium with footballs

...weigh a goldfish

...and meet an iceberg the size of Jamaica.

As well as finding out about size and what fits into what how many times, you might discover some unexpected facts about things like blue whales' earwax, the moons of Jupiter and kangaroos the size of grapes.

With elephants and mountains featuring in this book, you won't be surprised to hear that we'll be meeting some very, very big numbers. But don't let that worry you! There's a note about numbers by Murderous Maths legend Kjartan Poskitt on page 8, and his guide to different measurements and how to measure is on page 44.

Plus, as if all that weren't enough, you will be flying around at 1,000 km/h to some interesting destinations using your very own jetpack.

But first, turn the page and let Kjartan set your mind at rest about big numbers.

Say HELLO to BIG NUMBERS

By Kjartan Poskitt

Big numbers might look scary at first, but when you know how they work, they're fun!

Let's start by looking at a big number you might find at home. How many drops of water do you think it takes to fill a bath right to the top?

Let's look at the sums.

- 5,000 — five thousand
- 50,000 — fifty thousand
- 500,000 — five hundred thousand (which is half a million)
- 5,000,000 — five million

A full bath holds *about* 250 litres of water, and each litre of water is *about* 20,000 drops. Therefore the total number of drops in the bath is:

250 x 20,000 = 5,000,000

You'll notice we said *about*. When we play with very big numbers, we don't usually need to be absolutely accurate, and that means it makes the sums quite simple to do. The main thing is to make sure you have the right number of zeros!

When we work out 250 x 20,000, we first add up the number of zeros. We get 1 + 4 = five zeros. Remember that!

Now we ignore the zeros and just multiply the numbers at the front. 25 x 2 = 50. That's easy!

Now we just put our five zeros on the end of the 50. We get the answer 5000000, and, when you put the commas in, it becomes 5,000,000. So there are *about* five million drops of water in the bath!

Here are some more to take a guess at:

- What's longer – a million seconds or 1 year?
- What's taller – 100 giraffes or 1,000,000 ants?
- What's heavier – the water in an Olympic swimming pool or the Eiffel Tower?

You'll find the answers at the back of the book.

Using a Calculator

Calculators are really good for big sums *unless you push the wrong buttons.* It won't be the calculator's fault if you get the wrong answer! Therefore, it's always good to have a rough answer in your head and make sure the calculator agrees with you.

Suppose a bakery makes 873 packets of biscuits with 23 biscuits in each packet. How many biscuits is that altogether? The sum is 873 x 23 but which answer do you think is correct?

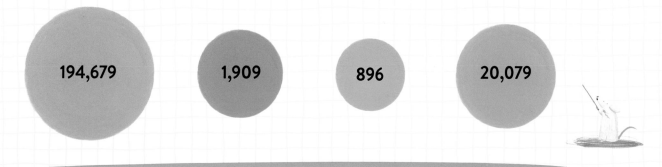

194,679   1,909   896   20,079

TO WORK IT OUT

The trick is to round the numbers off. 873 is nearly 1,000, which makes an easy multiplication: 1,000 x 23 = 23,000. So which answer is nearest? It's 20,079.
(What was wrong with the other answers? The first answer is 873 x 223, the second answer is 83 x 23 and the third is 873 + 23.)

It's fun guessing what the answer to a big sum will be, and then using a calculator to see how close you were. The more often you try it, the better you will be!

Playing around with big numbers tells us all sorts of amazing and crazy things. So, are you ready? Off we go then . . .

How Many mice Make an ELEPHANT?

You have probably already noticed that elephants are very big and mice are very small. In fact, African elephants are the biggest land animal in the world. But how many mice could you fit into one of these hefty, trumpeting stompers?

This enormous African elephant takes up around **6 million cubic centimetres** (cm³) of space, or **six cubic metres** (m³).

This little house mouse takes up around **25 cubic centimetres** (cm³) of space or **0.000025 cubic metres** (m³).

📟 TO WORK IT OUT

Divide six million (6,000,000) by 25. (Or **divide 6 by 0.000025** if you'd rather use cubic metres). Either way the result is the same.

You'd need 240,000 mice to fill up the space of just one elephant!

How Small is Our Mouse?

WEIGHT
about 25 grams

LENGTH
about 8 cm (body)
about 7 cm (tail)

one at a time

How Big is Our Elephant?

WEIGHT
about 6 tonnes, or 6,000,000 grams

HEIGHT
about 3.3 m

Even though they're tiny, house mice can jump up to 45 cm high. That's like you leaping up to the roof of a house. Elephants can't jump at all — they never have all four feet off the ground at the same time.

An elephant uses its trunk for lots of things, including sniffing, picking things up, sucking up water to drink, sucking up mud or sand for a bath, and giving other elephants a cuddle. The trunk has more than 40,000 muscles to help it do all these jobs. About 24 house mice could line up along an African elephant's trunk.

You could wrap yourself up inside an elephant's ear, which can measure 2 m across — as long as the elephant didn't mind, of course.

There are *billions* of house mice in the world, but not so many African elephants. Today there are about 415,000 African elephants in the wild, but 100 years ago there were more than three million of them.

How Many FLIGHTS of Stairs to the Top of MOUNT EVEREST?

Grab your crampons and an ice pick, because it's time to scale the highest mountain in the world. Obviously, it would be a lot easier if there were stairs to climb to the top, but how many flights would we need?

The flight of stairs in our imaginary house is **2.5 m** high.

Mount Everest is **8,848 m** high.

We would need **3,539 FLIGHTS OF STAIRS** (plus a few steps) to climb Mount Everest!

IS THERE A LIFT?

TO WORK IT OUT

Divide 8,848 by 2.5

Here is the highest peak on each continent, along with the number of flights of stairs needed to climb it. Australia's Mount Kosciuszko is just a hill compared to Everest!

1. **ASIA:** Mount Everest 8,848 m		(**3,539** flights of stairs)
2. **SOUTH AMERICA:** Aconcagua 6,962 m		(**2,785** flights of stairs)
3. **NORTH AMERICA:** Denali 6,190 m		(**2,476** flights of stairs)
4. **AFRICA:** Mount Kilimanjaro 5,895 m		(**2,358** flights of stairs)
5. **EUROPE:** Mount Elbrus 5,642 m		(**2,257** flights of stairs)
6. **ANTARCTICA:** Vinson Massif 4,892 m		(**1,957** flights of stairs)
7. **AUSTRALIA:** Mount Kosciuszko 2,228 m		(**891** flights of stairs)

All five of the world's highest peaks are found in the Himalaya mountain range, which includes more than 50 peaks that are higher than 7,200 m, and ten over 8,000 m.

Mount Everest was climbed for the first time in 1953 (at least, the first time it was recorded). Since then there have been more than 7,000 ascents, and there are hundreds more every year.

May and June are the only months that weather allows climbers to reach Everest's summit, and sometimes there's a long queue of mountaineers waiting to get there!

The Himalayas formed when two massive plates in the Earth's crust collided with one another, joining India, which used to be a very big island off the coast of Australia, with Asia. India drifted slowly northwards until it crashed into Asia about 40 to 50 million years ago.

How many swimming pools in the SEA?

There's more ocean in the world than there is land, and, while some of it is shallow enough to paddle in, a great deal of it is very deep indeed. Just how much seawater is sloshing about on planet Earth compared to how much there is in a pool?

We're using an **Olympic-sized swimming pool**, which contains **2,500 m³** of water.

There's a lot of water in the sea — around **1,400,000,000,000,000,000 m³**. (That's 1,400 million billion m³)

There are 560,000,000,000,000 (THAT'S 560 TRILLION) swimming pools' worth of water in the sea!

 TO WORK IT OUT

Divide 1,400,000,000,000,000,000 by 2,500 (there are too many zeros to fit on a calculator, so use the zero counting method on page 8, but subtract zeros rather than add them.)

Unlike a swimming pool, the sea is salty – the salt comes from rocks on land as rainwater erodes them and washes into the sea, and also from minerals in geothermal vents on the sea floor.

On average, the sea is 3.6 km deep, but the deepest part is the Mariana Trench in the Pacific Ocean. The deepest area of the trench, called Challenger Deep, is nearly 11 km (or more than 13 Burj Khalifa skyscrapers – see pages 16-17) below the sea's surface. Three expeditions have been made to the freezing, dark, bone-crushingly pressurized trench – the latest in 2019.

MOUNT EVEREST WOULD COME UP TO HERE

Although the oceans all join up, they're usually divided into four main oceans – the Pacific, Atlantic, Indian and Arctic. Some people call the water around Antarctica the Southern Ocean, making five in total.

30%

The ocean is our planet's largest habitat, covering 70% of its surface.

The Pacific Ocean is the biggest – it contains half of all the seawater on Earth.

If the base of **Mount Everest** was at the bottom of the **Mariana Trench**, there would be more than **2 km of clear water** above the top of the mountain.

HOW many GIRAFFES make the tallest SKYSCRAPER?

We're using this lovely giraffe. She's called Gillian and she's **4.6 m** tall.

TO WORK IT OUT

Divide 828 by 4.6

If you're afraid of heights you might need to close your eyes and hang on to something sturdy. How many giraffes would have to stand on top of one another to get to the top of the world's tallest building?

The Burj Khalifa is the world's tallest building – it's a dizzying **828 m** tall.

You'd need **180 GILLIAN-SIZED GIRAFFES**, stacked very uncomfortably one on top of the other, to reach the TOP OF THE BURJ KHALIFA.

Giraffes are the world's tallest mammals, between about 4 m and 6 m tall. Just their necks are longer than most grown-ups, and their blue tongues can measure more than 50 cm.

The World's Tallest Buildings Measured in Giraffes

1. **BURJ KHALIFA,** United Arab Emirates — **180 GIRAFFES** (828 m)
2. **SHANGHAI TOWER,** China — **137 GIRAFFES** (632 m)
3. **MAKKAH ROYAL CLOCK TOWER,** Saudi Arabia — **131 GIRAFFES** (601 m)
4. **PING AN FINANCE CENTRE,** China — **130 GIRAFFES** (599 m)
5. **LOTTE WORLD TOWER,** Korea — **120 GIRAFFES** (554.5 m)

(Giraffe numbers have been rounded up or down – no giraffes have been harmed in the making of this book.)

From 1931 until 1972, the world's tallest building was the Empire State Building in New York City, at 381 m, or 83 Gillians. You could stack two Empire State Buildings on top of one another and still have 66 m left to reach the top of the Burj Khalifa. New technology and lighter building materials mean buildings keep getting higher and higher.

The Burj Khalifa has to cope with the wind, like all tall buildings, and also with salty water in the ground that could damage its foundations. So its base is spread over a wide area, and its deep, concrete-and-metal foundations are resistant to salt water.

Steel frames help to support the thousands of tonnes that today's tall buildings weigh.

How many SANDPITS in the SAHARA DESERT?

The Sahara is the world's biggest sandy desert, and is almost as big as China. If all the sand somehow blew away suddenly, how many sandpits would we need to refill it?

> There's roughly **200 trillion m³ (200,000,000,000,000 m³)** of sand in the Sahara (a trillion is a million millions).

> This lovely sandpit contains **2 m³** of sand.

> DO YOU HAVE A BIGGER WHEELBARROW?

We need **100 TRILLION** (that's one followed by 14 zeros) sandpits to fill the Sahara. I hope you've got a wheelbarrow!

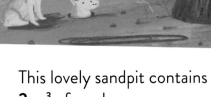

🖩 TO WORK IT OUT

Divide **200,000,000,000,000 by 2** (there are too many zeros to fit on a calculator, so use the zero counting method on page 8, but subtract the zeros rather than add them.)

The Sahara is 9.2 million km² of dry dusty desert. The island of Mauritius off the coast of Africa could fit into it 4,600 times! Most of the Sahara is gravelly and rocky, with mountains up to 3,400 m high, but there's still plenty of sand – around 2 million km² (which we're saying is 100 m deep on average to come up with our volume).

Saharan sand dunes are called ergs and can be 180 m high, though that's nowhere near the tallest in the world. The tallest can measure over 1,000 m!

The Sahara has extreme temperatures: it's often around 38°C during the day, but the highest temperature ever recorded was 58°C. On winter nights the temperature can fall below freezing.

Anywhere on Earth that gets less than 250 mm of rain in a year is a desert, so not all deserts are hot and sandy. The biggest ones of all are Antarctica and the Arctic, planet Earth's cold poles.

Some Very Big Deserts

. . . and how many times the country of France could fit into them

1.	SAHARA	**9.2 MILLION** km² (just over 14.5 x France)
2.	ARABIAN	**2.3 MILLION** km² (just over 3.5 x France)
3.	GOBI	**1.3 MILLION** km² (just over 2 x France)
4.	KALAHARI	**900,000** km² (just over 1.6 x France)
5.	PATAGONIAN	**620,000** km² (just over 1.1 x France)

How high HIGH JUMPS to the MOON?

Even the world-record-holding high jumper couldn't get anywhere near the Moon, which is quite a long way away. But how many jumps would it take?

The distance to the Moon varies quite a bit, but a rough average is about **385,000 km,** or **385,000,000 (385 million) m**.

The world record high jump is **2.45 m** (jumped by Javier Sotomayor from Cuba in 1993).

On average, the Moon is **157,142,857 AND A BIT HIGH JUMPS AWAY** from Earth! Only nursery rhyme cows are capable of jumping over it.

TO WORK IT OUT

Divide 385,000,000 by 2.45

It's just as well we don't have to rely on jumping to get into space – we use rockets to zoom us up there instead. During the 1960s and 70s NASA's Apollo programme sent nine missions to the Moon, and altogether twelve astronauts have walked on its surface.

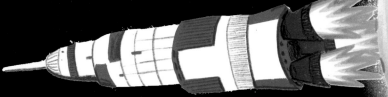

Moons in Our Solar System

Earth only has one moon, but some planets in our solar system have lots.

- MERCURY AND VENUS: 0
- EARTH: 1
- MARS: 2
- JUPITER: 79 (the biggest planet also has the biggest moon, Ganymede)
- SATURN: at least 82 (astronomers keep finding more and more!)
- URANUS: 27
- NEPTUNE: 14

The Moon is roughly a quarter of the size of Earth at 3,476 km in diameter. If you hollowed out the Earth, there would be room for about 50 of our Moons (if they were all squashed in).

The Moon has only one-sixth of Earth's gravity, so you'd weigh a lot less and be able to jump six times higher on the Moon. If Sotomayor had completed his record-breaking jump on the Moon instead of on Earth, he could have jumped over a three-storey building.

Human high-jumping efforts are pathetically puny compared to how high some animals can jump. White-tailed jackrabbits have been recorded jumping as high as 6.4 m, which would be like you jumping over a giraffe.

Fleas jump up to 200 times their body length – like you jumping over 30 London buses parked end to end.

HOW MANY KANGAROO HOPS to cross AUSTRALIA?

Australia is the name of a continent as well as a country. Kangaroos are some of its most famous animals, known for their awesome hopping abilities. If a kangaroo started hopping across the whole of Australia, how many hops would it need to do?

Our red kangaroo covers **7.5 m** in one hop.

The distance across Australia from east to west is roughly **4,000 km**, or **4,000,000 m**.

It would take 533,333 (and a bit) KANGAROO HOPS TO CROSS AUSTRALIA. Maybe lots of kangaroos could do it in a relay.

 TO WORK IT OUT

Divide 4,000,000 by 7.5

As well as covering 7.5 m across the ground, a red kangaroo's hop can reach 1.8 m high – it could jump over you with no problem at all. A kangaroo can reach speeds of up to 56 km/h as it bounds along, breaking the speed limit in a built-up area.

The World's Four Widest Countries Measured in Kangaroo Hops

Australia isn't the widest country in the world – Canada is. You could fit more than two Australias, side by side, east to west, across the width of Canada. All the following numbers are just rough estimates. Especially for the kangaroos.

1. **Canada** 1.24 million kangaroo hops (9,360 km wide)
2. **Russia** 1.2 million kangaroo hops (9,000 km wide)
3. **China** 693,000 kangaroo hops (5,200 km wide)
4. **USA** 597,333 kangaroo hops (4,480 km wide)

Marsupials are a type of mammal. After a baby marsupial is born, it lives in its mother's pouch until it's bigger. The red kangaroo is the biggest marsupial of the lot. A baby red kangaroo is only the size of a grape when it's born, but it grows into a whopping great hopper with a body length of up to 1.6 m, plus a tail that's more than 1 m long.

The main bit of Australia is an island, but it also includes other smaller islands too. The biggest is Tasmania, which is 300 km, or 40,000 kangaroo hops, from east to west.

How many ICE CUBES make an ICEBERG?

Icebergs are enormous chunks of ice floating in the sea or a lake. Ice cubes are for keeping your lemonade cold. But they're both made of the same thing – frozen water. We know icebergs are big, but how many ice cubes make one?

Our medium-sized iceberg is about the size of a big house at **400 m³**, or **400,000,000 cm³** (that's **400 million cm³**).

Our ice cubes have a volume of **25 cm³**.

There are **16 MILLION ICE CUBES IN OUR ICEBERG.** You could keep everyone in New Zealand's drinks cold with that.

 TO WORK IT OUT

Divide 400,000,000 by 25. We are going to need quite a lot of ice cubes.

A chunk of floating ice is called an iceberg once it's bigger than 5 m across. Chunks of floating ice that are smaller than that are known as bergy bits and growlers. You'll notice that most of our iceberg is underwater, and this is true of all of them – usually you can only see about a tenth of an iceberg above the surface.

Icebergs come in different shapes and sizes, from house-sized chunks to ice islands. They form when they break off from glaciers, which are huge rivers of ice that flow very slowly across land.

Ice floats in water because it isn't as dense as liquid water. Icebergs are made from freshwater, which is less dense than salty seawater, and that helps them float, too.

Most glaciers are found in Greenland and Antarctica. Around 13.5 million km² of Antarctica is covered in glaciers, and if all of them melted, sea levels would rise by about 58 m. Sea levels are rising, partly because of ice melting as the Earth's climate gets warmer.

Iceberg B-15 was the biggest iceberg ever recorded. It measured nearly 300 km long and 37 km wide – bigger than the island of Jamaica.

How many Christmas Trees make a coast REDWOOD?

Coast redwoods are the tallest trees in the world, and you will probably be surprised at just how tall they can get. Christmas trees need to be small enough to fit inside your house. How many small trees would you have to stand on top of one another to reach the top of a great big one?

Our Christmas tree is **2 m** tall (and quite honestly that's a bit on the big side for our living room).

This is the tallest coast redwood alive today, which also makes it the tallest tree alive today. It's **116 m** tall.

We need 58 CHRISTMAS TREES to reach the top of the coast redwood!

TO WORK IT OUT

Divide 116 by 2

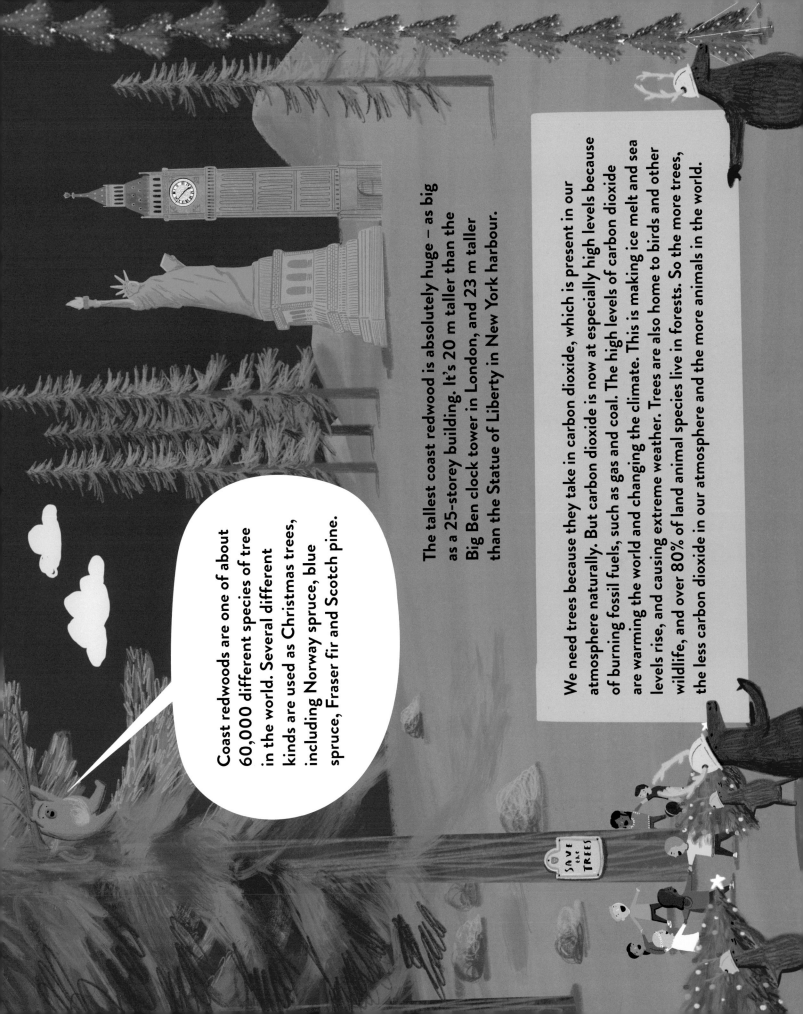

Coast redwoods are one of about 60,000 different species of tree in the world. Several different kinds are used as Christmas trees, including Norway spruce, blue spruce, Fraser fir and Scotch pine.

The tallest coast redwood is absolutely huge — as big as a 25-storey building. It's 20 m taller than the Big Ben clock tower in London, and 23 m taller than the Statue of Liberty in New York harbour.

We need trees because they take in carbon dioxide, which is present in our atmosphere naturally. But carbon dioxide is now at especially high levels because of burning fossil fuels, such as gas and coal. The high levels of carbon dioxide are warming the world and changing the climate. This is making ice melt and sea levels rise, and causing extreme weather. Trees are also home to birds and other wildlife, and over 80% of land animal species live in forests. So the more trees, the less carbon dioxide in our atmosphere and the more animals in the world.

SAVE the TREES

How many PLANET EARTHS FIT inside the SUN?

The Sun doesn't look all that big from here on Earth. But, as you've probably already worked out, that's because it's a really long way away. How much bigger is it than planet Earth, and just how far away is it?

I thought it would be BIGGER.

The volume of the Sun is about
1,400,000,000,000,000,000 km³
(1,400 million billion km³).

The volume of Earth is about
1,000,000,000,000 km³ (a trillion km³).

About **1,400,000 EARTHS** would fit inside the Sun (you would have to reduce them to rubble and goo first, though).

TO WORK IT OUT

Divide 1,400,000,000,000,000,000 by 1,000,000,000,000 (there are too many zeros to fit on a calculator, so use the zero counting method on page 8.)

Our Sun is absolutely huge, but it's only medium-sized as far as stars go – there are stars more than 100 times wider.

The smallest planet in our solar system is Mercury, which is about one third the diameter of Earth.

SPACE TOURS

The Sun is our nearest star. The Earth and all the other planets in our solar system (eight altogether) are in orbit around it. In order from closest to the Sun, they are: Mercury, Venus, Earth, Mars, Jupiter, Saturn, Uranus and Neptune.

The Sun is about 150 million km away from Earth which is known as an Astronomical Unit (AU). Sometimes scientists talk about very large distances in AUs

The biggest planet is Jupiter, which is about 1,300 times bigger than Earth – in fact, all the other planets in the solar system could fit inside Jupiter. But you could still fit 1,000 Jupiters inside the Sun!

How Big is the Earth?

Planet Earth is about 40,000 km measured all the way around the middle (its circumference). Travelling at 1,000 km per hour in a very fast plane, it would take 40 hours to fly all the way around it.

The Sun's circumference measures about 4,400,000 km. Travelling all the way around the Sun in a very fast plane would take six months. If you lined up 109 planet Earths in a row, it would be equal to the diameter of the Sun.

How Many FOOTBALLS fill the World's BIGGEST STADIUM?

Have you ever wondered how many footballs would fill a stadium if you took out all the seats and changing rooms and things? Of course you hav

A football has a diameter of **22 cm**. We're not going to squash the balls so there's no space between them, but if we just chuck them in and allow them to nestle together, there will be about **133 footballs in one cubic metre (1 m³).**

The biggest stadium in the world is Rungrado May Day Stadium in North Korea. Very roughly, its volume is **1,000,000 m³ (1 million m³).**

133,000,000 FOOTBALLS would fill up the **WORLD'S BIGGEST STADIUM.**

TO WORK IT OUT

Multiply 1 million by 133

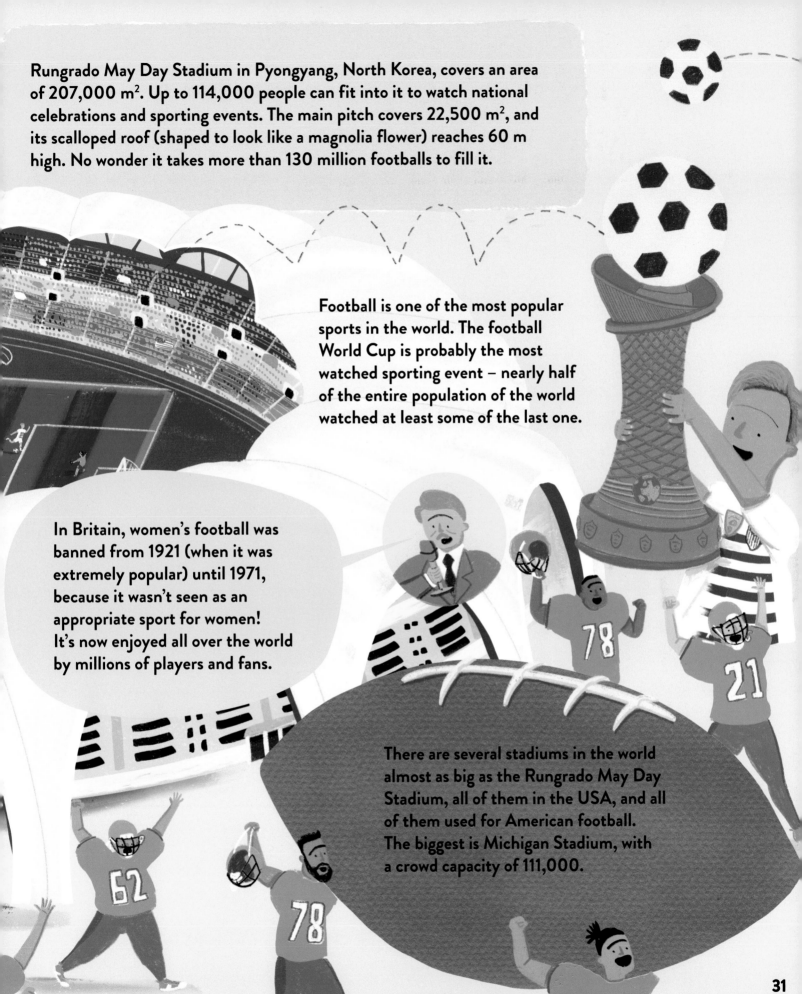

Rungrado May Day Stadium in Pyongyang, North Korea, covers an area of 207,000 m². Up to 114,000 people can fit into it to watch national celebrations and sporting events. The main pitch covers 22,500 m², and its scalloped roof (shaped to look like a magnolia flower) reaches 60 m high. No wonder it takes more than 130 million footballs to fill it.

Football is one of the most popular sports in the world. The football World Cup is probably the most watched sporting event – nearly half of the entire population of the world watched at least some of the last one.

In Britain, women's football was banned from 1921 (when it was extremely popular) until 1971, because it wasn't seen as an appropriate sport for women! It's now enjoyed all over the world by millions of players and fans.

There are several stadiums in the world almost as big as the Rungrado May Day Stadium, all of them in the USA, and all of them used for American football. The biggest is Michigan Stadium, with a crowd capacity of 111,000.

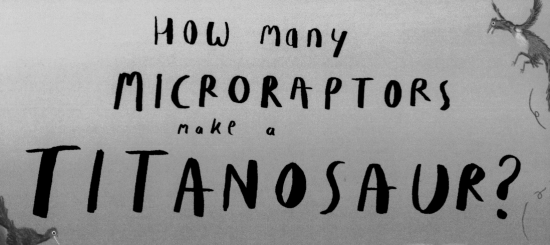

HOW many MICRORAPTORS make a TITANOSAUR?

Not all dinosaurs were huge lumbering monsters – these ancient beasts came in all sorts of shapes and sizes. How many of the smallest would weigh the same as the biggest?

Titanosaurs are the largest kind of dinosaur we know about. Ours weighed about **70 tonnes (or 70,000 kg)**.

Microraptor, one of the smallest types of dinosaur, weighed about **1 kg**.

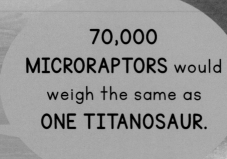

70,000 MICRORAPTORS would weigh the same as ONE TITANOSAUR.

 TO WORK IT OUT

Divide 70,000 by 1. This is an easy one!

There were different kinds of microraptor – little feathered dinosaurs about the size of crows that preyed on smaller animals. One of them, Microraptor gui, had feathers adapted for flight on all four of its limbs. It could probably fly, or at least glide.

Our big dinosaur is a titanosaur, a type of sauropod, which were huge plant-eaters. This titanosaur is a type called Argentinosaurus, which is thought to be not only the largest dinosaur, but the largest known land animal in the world ever. It measured 35 m from head to tail.

Elephants are the biggest land animals in the world today. Eleven of the very biggest African elephants would make one Argentinosaurus.

Compsognathus was one of the smallest non-flying dinosaurs – a little 65-cm-long meat-eater. It was about three times as heavy as a microraptor, so we'd need 23,300 or so of those to make one Argentinosaurus.

Microraptors and titanosaurs would never have met because they were separated by millions of years. Microraptors lived about 125 million years ago, while titanosaurs lived towards the end of the age of the dinosaurs. Argentinosaurus lived around 90 million years ago.

The biggest meat-eating dinosaur fossil discovered so far is a Tyrannosaurus rex called Scotty, found in 2019. It measures 13 m long and would have weighed 8,800 kg when it was alive – or 8,800 microraptors if you'd rather.

How many Central Parks make the AMAZON RAINFOREST?

The Amazon is the biggest tropical rainforest in the world, and it is very big indeed. Central Park in New York City is one of the most famous parks in the world. How many of one would fit inside the other?

Central Park is **3.4 km²**.

The Amazon covers an area of about **5.5 million km²**.

You could fit 1,617,647 CENTRAL PARKS INSIDE THE AMAZON RAINFOREST. Incidentally, the Amazon is roughly half the size of Europe.

 TO WORK IT OUT
Divide 5,500,000 by 3.4

Most of the Amazon rainforest is in Brazil, but it covers parts of seven other countries in South America: Bolivia, Colombia, Ecuador, French Guiana, Guyana, Peru and Suriname. Suriname is the smallest country in South America at 163,820 km^2 – it could fit into the Amazon rainforest more than 30 times.

The Amazon is home to millions of different animals and plants. There are more than 2.5 million kinds of insect, more than 400 types of mammal, and thousands of types of fish and birds.

Tropical rainforests are hot and humid, with more than 2 m of rainfall per year and an average temperature higher than 28°C.

Among the extraordinary animals living in the Amazon are the world's biggest beetle, the titan beetle, and the world's smallest monkey, the pygmy marmoset.

Central Park includes a reservoir, a huge museum, a lake, various ponds and pools, a theatre, a zoo and even a castle. But obviously it's absolutely titchy compared to the world's biggest rainforest.

Rainforests are beautiful and also useful to the planet, because they absorb carbon dioxide and release oxygen, which helps to stabilize the climate. Sadly, an area of the Amazon more than four and a half times the size of Suriname has been destroyed in the last 50 years, mostly to make way for grazing land for cattle.

How many ASTRONAUTS fit inside the INTERNATIONAL SPACE STATION?

The International Space Station (ISS) is in orbit about 400 km above the Earth. How many astronauts are whizzing about up there with it, and how many more could fit inside?

The crew of the ISS is usually six astronauts. But what if we wanted to squash them in? We wouldn't really be that cruel, but just out of interest . . .

The ISS has a volume (where it's possible to live) of **388 m³**.

An average astronaut takes up around **0.065 m³**.

5,969 ASTRONAUTS COULD FIT INSIDE THE INTERNATIONAL SPACE STATION. That's 5,963 more than the usual crew. Each bedroom would have to be shared by nearly a thousand astronauts.

TO WORK IT OUT
Divide 388 by 0.065

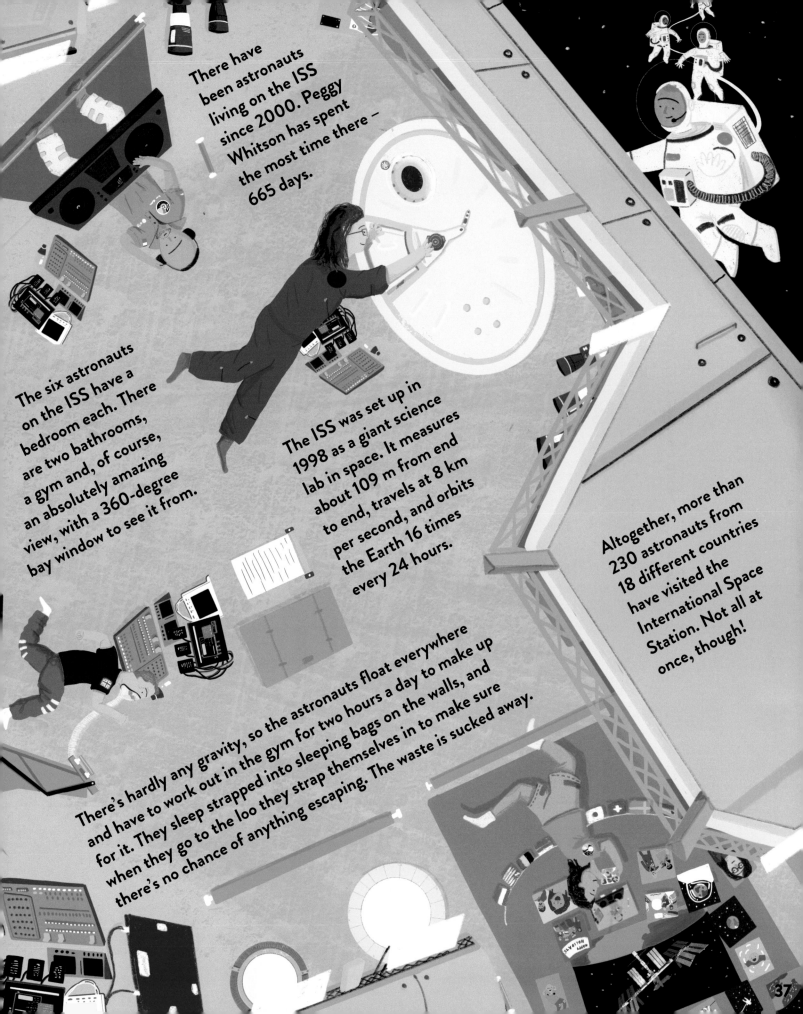

There have been astronauts living on the ISS since 2000. Peggy Whitson has spent the most time there – 665 days.

The six astronauts on the ISS have a bedroom each. There are two bathrooms, a gym and, of course, an absolutely amazing view, with a 360-degree bay window to see it from.

The ISS was set up in 1998 as a giant science lab in space. It measures about 109 m from end to end, travels at 8 km per second, and orbits the Earth 16 times every 24 hours.

Altogether, more than 230 astronauts from 18 different countries have visited the International Space Station. Not all at once, though!

There's hardly any gravity, so the astronauts float everywhere and have to work out in the gym for two hours a day to make up for it. They sleep strapped into sleeping bags on the walls, and when they go to the loo they strap themselves in to make sure there's no chance of anything escaping. The waste is sucked away.

HOW many goldfish make a BLUE WHALE?

Blue whales are the biggest animals that have ever existed on Earth. Obviously, goldfish are teeny tiny by comparison. But how many of these little tiddlers would weigh the same as a whopping great blue whale?

A blue whale can weigh up to **200 metric tonnes**, or 200,000,000 (200 million) grams.

Goldfish vary in size, but our one, called Graham, weighs **400 grams.**

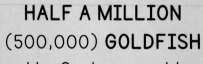

HALF A MILLION (500,000) GOLDFISH like Graham would weigh the same as one blue whale!

 TO WORK IT OUT

Divide 200,000,000 by 400

Often goldfish are kept in small tanks, but if they're given a nice big tank to swim around in they'll grow bigger and be happier.

You can tell a blue whale's age from its earwax. Around every six months, a new layer of earwax forms. These 'earplugs' tell scientists that blue whales usually live between 80 to 90 years. The oldest on record lived about 110 years.

Blue whales eat tiny creatures called krill – up to four tonnes of them a day. Goldfish will eat almost anything, including their own poo. They will keep eating and eating, because they don't have a stomach and can't tell when they're full.

ALL YOU CAN EAT!

When a blue whale is born, it already weighs nearly 2 tonnes, or 5,000 goldfish. When it's fully grown, it measures up to 30 m long – 200 Graham-sized goldfish could line up along it.

A blue whale's tongue weighs as much as a rhinoceros, and its heart is the size of a car.

Goldfish are freshwater fish, so they woudn't meet a blue whale in real life. They're a type of carp, originally from east Asia.

Goldfish are famous for only being able to remember things for a few seconds, but that's not true. They can identify shapes, colours and sounds, and they can be taught to do tricks like pushing balls through hoops.

The world's biggest goldfish weighed 900 grams and measured 32 cm, but most don't reach anywhere near that size.

How many football Pitches to cover PLANET EARTH?

The last time you were watching an especially exciting cup match, you were probably wondering just how many of those pitches it would take to cover the entire planet. In between goals, obviously.

The surface area of Earth is about **510,000,000 (510 million) km²**. A lot of that is under the sea, so if we're talking about dry land, the area is about **150 million km²**.

Football pitches can be different sizes, but our one measures 120 m long by 70 m wide, which is an area of **8,400 m², or 0.0084 km².**

We'd need **60,714,285,714** and a bit of our **FOOTBALL PITCHES TO COVER THE WHOLE OF PLANET EARTH.**

TO COVER THE WORLD'S DRY LAND, we would need **17,857,142,857** and a bit of our football pitches.

 TO WORK IT OUT

Divide 510,000,000 by 0.0084
To work it out for just the land area
divide 150,000,000 by 0.0084

The Earth's crust is made up of great big chunks called tectonic plates. Millions of years ago, the plates were all joined together in one huge supercontinent. Then they drifted apart, and made mountains as they crashed together again.

How Many Football Pitches Would Cover . . .

THE ENTIRE OCEAN:
42,857,142,857

THE WORLD'S LARGEST LAKE: (Caspian Sea) 44,166,666

THE WORLD'S BIGGEST COUNTRY: (Russia)
2,032,761,285

THE WORLD'S SMALLEST COUNTRY: (the Vatican)
You'd need just 52.4 football pitches, because the Vatican is really very small indeed.

Some Football Numbers . . .

There are more nations with football teams than any other sport – there are 211 national men's teams, and 176 national women's teams. Football is the most popular team sport played by women.

Jetpack JOURNEYS

By this stage in the book, you are probably wondering what on earth has happened to the jetpack you were promised. At last, here it is! Put it on and get ready to fly to destinations around the world – and beyond – at 1,000 km/h.

You might have already flown at 1,000 km/h – passenger planes sometimes reach that speed.

Cross-country Journeys:

ACROSS CANADA FROM EAST TO WEST (widest point): 9.5 hours

ACROSS CHINA FROM EAST TO WEST (widest point): 5.25 hours

ACROSS THE UNITED STATES FROM EAST TO WEST (widest point): 4.5 hours

ACROSS BRAZIL FROM EAST TO WEST (widest point): 4.2 hours

ACROSS MAINLAND ITALY FROM NORTH TO SOUTH (widest point): 1.2 hours

City to City Journeys:

NEW YORK, USA TO LONDON, UK: 5.5 hours

DELHI, INDIA TO SYDNEY, AUSTRALIA: 10.5 hours

BEIJING, CHINA TO PARIS, FRANCE: 8.25 hours

LAGOS, NIGERIA TO PRETORIA, SOUTH AFRICA: 4.5 hours

BERLIN, GERMANY TO LOS ANGELES, USA: 9.25 hours

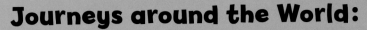

Journeys around the World:

WORLD'S LONGEST RAILWAY (THE TRANS-SIBERIAN RAILWAY): 9.25 hours

THE GREAT WALL OF CHINA: 21.25 hours

THE RIVER NILE: 6.75 hours

THE PACIFIC OCEAN (FROM EAST TO WEST AT WIDEST POINT): 19.75 hours

THE ATLANTIC OCEAN: 6.5 hours

Space Journeys from Earth to:

THE MOON: 2 weeks, 2 days and half an hour

MARS (AT CLOSEST POINT): 6 years, 11 weeks, 3 days and 2 hours

THE SUN: 17 years, 3 weeks, 3 days and just under two hours

JUPITER (AT CLOSEST POINT): 71 years, 37 weeks, 5 days and 21 hours

NEPTUNE (AT CLOSEST POINT): 490 years, 27 weeks, 5 days and 4 hours

Measuring Different Things

By Kjartan Poskitt

We use different units depending on what we're measuring.

> The base unit is 1 metre (which you can write as 1 m).
>
> We use metres for measuring lines or distances.
>
> 1 m is about as long as a belt or the height of a table top.

There are 100 centimetres (100 cm) in 1 metre. 1 cm is about the width of a pea.

There are 1,000 millimetres (1,000 mm) in 1 metre. 1 mm is about the thickness of ten pieces of paper.

1,000 metres = 1 kilometre (or 1 km). That's about as far as you can walk in 10 minutes.

If we need to measure the size of areas such as a carpet or the surface of the Earth, we use square metres (m²) or square kilometres (km²) for big areas.

1 metre

1 metre

1 metre

A square with sides a metre long is 1 square metre (1 m²).

1 metre

One square metre (1 m²) is about half the size of a door in an ordinary house.

One square centimetre (1 cm²) is about the size of your little fingernail.

One square millimetre (1 mm²) is about the size of a big full stop.

1 metre

1 metre

1 metre

A cube with sides a metre long is 1 cubic metre (1 m³).

If we need to measure the size of lumpy things such as footballs or elephants, these are volumes and we use cubic metres (m³). One cubic metre is about the size of a big washing machine.

One cubic millimetre (1 mm³) is the size of a grain of sugar.

One cubic centimetre (1 cm³) is the size of a small dice.

Index

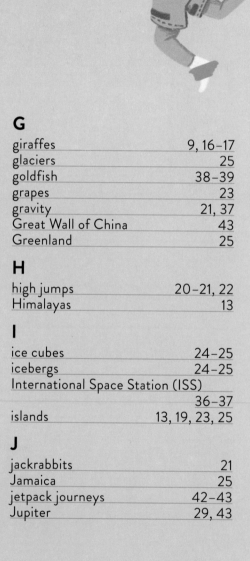

Answers to page 9:
One year = about 31.5 million seconds

1,000,000 ants = 2,000 m, 100 giraffes = 500 m

Eiffel Tower = 10,000 tonnes, pool water = 2,500 tonnes